Cracks in the Invisible

Cracks in the Invisible

poems

Stephen Kampa

OHIO UNIVERSITY PRESS

ATHENS

Ohio University Press, Athens, Ohio 45701
www.ohioswallow.com
© 2011 by Stephen Kampa

To obtain permission to quote, reprint, or otherwise reproduce or distribute material
from Ohio University Press publications, please contact our rights and permissions
department at (740) 593-1154 or (740) 593-4536 (fax).

Printed in the United States of America
Ohio University Press books are printed on acid-free paper ⊗ ™

20 19 18 17 16 15 14 13 12 11   5 4 3 2 1

Library of Congress Cataloging-in-Publication Data
Kampa, Stephen, 1981–
 Cracks in the invisible : poems / Stephen Kampa.
   p. cm.
 ISBN 978-0-8214-1952-6 (pbk.: alk. paper)
 I. Title.
PS3611.A469C73 2011
811'.6—dc22
                          2010054475

. . . my firstfruits for my Maker.

Acknowledgments

Grateful acknowledgment is made to the editors of the following journals where these poems, sometimes in earlier versions, first found homes:

Birmingham Poetry Review: "Mirror Image," "The Therapist on Teleology"

The Hopkins Review: sections II and III of "Domestic Operetta for One Voice" (titled "Cleaning House"), "Message on a Bottle"

Measure: "Organic Decomposition" (titled "Sinful Roots")

River Styx: "*Dracula* in Spanish: Imitations of Immortality," "Streetlight and Stars"

The Sewanee Theological Review: "Elegy for Paul deLay," "Nocturne in the Key of Water," "Reading *Pilgrim's Progress* While Waiting to Be Tested for STDs"

Smartish Pace: "An Anatomy of Autonomy"

The Southwest Review: "Phenomena, Numina, Startling Sparrows," "Soul"

Subtropics: "The Reclamation of Paradise," "Upon Finishing *Don Juan*"

Unsplendid.com: "Not at the Grave of Dylan Thomas," "Twenty-First-Century Prothalamion"

My gratitude belongs to so many people in so many places. I am grateful to my family, and especially to my parents, for encouraging me to pursue poetry and music despite the obvious financial impracticability of these pursuits. I owe thanks to many friends, but most especially to Scott Durden, whose support has been immeasurable and whose friendship continues to astonish me with gladness. I have also been blessed with incomparable teachers, including Teresina Lyman, who first brought me to poetry; Greg Hewett and Constance Walker at Carleton College; and John Irwin, Mary Jo Salter, Dave Smith, and Greg Williamson at the Johns Hopkins University. I offer special thanks to Mary Jo: no one should have to read as many drafts as she read, and no one else could have done it with such grace, kindness, and sound poetic sense. A word of gratitude to each of the fine folks at the Sewanee Writers' Conference—staff, faculty, and participants alike. Innumerable thanks to Mark Jarman for his generosity and enthusiasm in reading my work, and to David Sanders for editorial wisdom and patience. I am indebted to Rossi Gannon and Harley Smith for generous permission to use the striking photograph on the cover. Most of all, my thanks to the God who sees me a long way off and comes running.

Contents

Aperture

Only be careful, and watch yourselves closely so that you do not forget the things your eyes have seen or let them slip from your heart as long as you live.

—*Deuteronomy* 4:9

Remember how
Bright galaxies of broken glass
Sparkle in parking lots
And seem to promise everlasting light,
Or how thin blades of grass
Stand patient guard on cemetery plots
Where everyone's an anchorite;
How even now

The dusky, cool
Breeze carries footsteps to your ear—
A husband climbing stairs
With penitential orchids in a vase,
Or crackheads drawing near
Their victim, jackknives flashing; how the cares
And joys are bound, face and efface
Both king and fool;

How every list
Suggests its own alternatives:
Etruscan, Hunnic, Manx
Recall all tongues no native speakers speak;
How common sense forgives
Sins one forgets (for this relief, much thanks);
And how each cheek evokes the cheek
That Judas kissed.

Do not omit
A single item you have read.
Remember Polyphemus
In Homer, Ovid, and Theocritus.
Recall the busy dead,
Translators of a world so polysemous
That even now most readers miss
The drift of it.

"There is in God
A deep, but dazzling darkness," Vaughan
Wrote (and "O, for thy centre!") —
Not the same darkness that couldn't comprehend
The living light in John,
But the thick darkness Moses had to enter
Before he met his promised end,
Buried abroad;

And as you dive
Into the realm of homonyms
And flat-five substitutions,
Contradistinctions, constant contradictions,
And misremembered hymns
("A wildness in God's mercy . . . "), no solutions
Will be forthcoming. Your convictions
May not survive.

Remember then
How an accordionist makes music —
Compressing and expanding
The bellows; how agglutination marks
The tongues of both Tungusic

And Finno-Ugric subgroups, notwithstanding
　　Their lexica; how God strikes sparks
　　　　From heart and pen;

　　　　How sequined sheets
　　Of dew can change to chain-mail shirts;
　　　　And how a distant laugh
Can well up at a bully's calling names
　　　　In bitter, spitfire spurts,
Or at the splendor of the cenotaph.
　　Surely whatever else it claims,
　　　　The world repeats

　　　　That all things mean.
　　Let the eidetic memory
　　　　Capture their grit and shine,
Remembering the aperture affects
　　　　The pictures' clarity.
Are their designs malignant or benign?
　　The evidence, in some respects,
　　　　Remains to be seen.

I. Sightings

To see is to forget; I never tire of such news.

—Donald Revell

Phenomena, Numina, Startling Sparrows

Faced with the world mistaken for the world,
I'm not confused: it seems so sensible
To call the loose, cyclonic pulse of leaves
On sidewalks "physics," and not a miracle.
I understand a prophet undeceives
Himself when, limping by the roadkill curled

Beside the curb, he thinks theodicy
Inadequate for even bestial pain,
Or when, dispersing the loud shroud of flies
That swaddles it, he wonders how the sane
Escape their own conclusions. Sense defies
Every compendium of mystery,

And if I'm senseless, then, for holding this
World most enlightening when its premises
Grow thinnest, I am glad to be struck dumb.
Look: fireflies punctuate the night with green
Epigrams on love, petunias keen
For the dead possum, and electrons hum

Concentric hymns to probability
While leaf-swirls sing in fractal harmony.
Best is this line of sparrows that have shown
Their utter distance from the disapproving
Caws of the crows by fleshing out a moving
Ellipsis leading into the unknown.

Theodicy

Sometimes you wake up inexplicably
Cheerful. Substantial reasons aren't the issue—
You have a queen-sized bed and clean beige sheets,
And over scrambled eggs you'll skim an issue
Of *Newsweek*, *The Economist*, or *Time*—
But that this blessing should be given time

And time again—not every day, but often
Enough to keep you from the chic despair
Young artists wear like an expensive watch—
Strikes you as something rich beyond compare.
This gladness almost makes up for the days
You stagger out the front door in a daze,

Having already called your spouse a name
That echoed through the kitchen like a dropped
Plate breaking; hours will pass, and you'll call home
Only to find your partner has graciously dropped
That morning's catastrophic argument
And pardoned you the words you never meant.

You'll leave the office happy, strolling past
A sunlight-rumpled bed of flame-bright phlox,
Which brings to mind an article you read:
It featured full-page pictures of huge flocks
Of crimson, pink, and even white flamingos.
Although you'd never cared about flamingos,

You browsed the "Fun Facts" boxes for the highlights:
Their color comes from beta carotene
Found in the food they filter from their mud-
And-water mouthfuls upside down; they preen
With arabesque contortions of their necks.
You pass a bus bench where a couple necks

Shamelessly in the open; farther down,
Your Eccos grind some broken picture-frame
Glass on the sidewalk, and you contemplate
Flamingos and a question you might frame:
You wonder if they're thinking when they look
At one another, *How beautiful you look!*

Somehow you know this deep, abiding joy
Only in part belongs to you: it comes
Unbidden. Maybe you'll make love tonight.
You love your life. You wonder if it comes,
This passion not created but begotten,
From something you've remembered or forgotten.

When the rain begins, I am two blocks down from
Meeting Grounds, a coffee shop/deli combo
(Almost always full) near the bend in Sixth Street,
    Just past Division.

Here and there, pedestrians start to open
Tabloids and umbrellas to keep from getting
Wet, but I've forgotten to bring a single
    Thing to protect me;

Splashing past a vagrant, I make a run for
Warmth, light, lox, and coffee with cream and sugar.
Someone holds the door for me. Here inside, rich
    Scents from the roasted

Coffee beans and lovingly baked panini
Rise to welcome all who have found this haven.
Windows flinch with raindrops the size of quarters.
    Patrons are tipping.

Just outside, the vagrant I passed is standing
Near the corner, cupping his hands together;
While the downpour fills them to overflowing,
    Servers behind me

Clear a vacant table. He lifts his hands to
Drink the ice-cold rain, and as soon as he has

Finished, there is more for his mouth. He doesn't
    Ask us for mercy,

Probably because he has seen our mercy
And instead prefers to accept the given
Rain, the sloppy handfuls of water, pure loose
    Change for a beggar,

Tossed to him directly by God, who loves him,
Numbers every thread of his coat, and gives him
So much more to keep him than, here and there, we
    Strangers have given.

Behold, I Come as a Thief

You could imagine God
Sliding his driver's license
Between the door and jamb
Or picking locks with hairpins,
Hoisting a bedroom window
And popping out the screen
Or posing as a plumber
To con the neighbor lady,
The one with the spare key,
Into allowing him
To enter your apartment
So when, at last, you open
Your own front door, arms full
Of groceries and the mail,
There God is, sitting at
The kitchen table, smiling,
Eating pecans or playing
A hand of solitaire;
He says, "Been waiting here
All afternoon," and gestures
To dirty dishes stacked
Next to the sink (and now
You can't remember whether
You left them there or God
Just made himself at home
While you were gone), and you
Stammer, "I didn't know
That you were on your way,"

And he says, "Follow me,"
And you two leave the building,
Using the fire escape
For secrecy, and slide
Into the back of a black
Rust-bucket station wagon
(God is the poorest gangster
You've ever seen), and he says
"Head to the overlook,"
And God, who's driving, snorts
"You got it," and the silence
During the ride unnerves you,
And finally the car
Swerves to a stop in a cloud
Of mesa dust, and God
Is waiting there, his hands
Behind his back, his feet
Tapping—he doesn't seem
Impatient, it's as though
He's listening to music,
A prelude you can't hear—
And you stumble from the car;
The God who has been waiting
Mumbles apologies
For spiriting you away
Without a warning, then
He says, "I want to show you
Something," and gestures downward—
The view blackberry-black
Except for pointillist clusters
Of light from houselights, streetlights,
Headlights and neon signs

That perforate the darkness—
And as the four of you
Stand awkwardly up there,
Those tiny points appear
To explode, rippling light
Outward until the scene
Looks almost like a photo
Negative of itself:
The landscape has become
An incandescent gold
So bright it could be white
Or blue, and what it makes
You think of are the words
You've never heard correctly
Used even once on earth—
Pure, righteous—and you feel
Unworthy now because
You know you shouldn't be
Able to look at this,
This adamantine brilliance
Hinting that holiness
Means always being apart
From God, who radiates
Joy at the sight of all
This light, and you, ashamed,
Cover your face, start crying,
And you say, "Oh, my God,"
And God, all ears, says, "Yes?"

Oracle from the Throat of the Cornucopia

Let gravitas-mongers disperse . . .

—John Holloway

Not yet. Let gravitas-
Mongers continue sales this afternoon
Here where the joyful villagers will soon
    Invest in bits of gravitas
Because their lives are otherwise complete:
Their sitcoms sparkle, Volvos growl, heart valves last longer,
    So now the villagers must all entreat
        The gnarled gravitas-monger.

"Sir," they exclaim, "we feel
Almost unbearably happy! Sell us wares
To rein our joy in; settle us with cares;
    Make our unbroken world seem real."
The gravitas-monger grabs each buyer's hand,
Touches the inside of the wrist, and rasps a phrase
    Like a struck match; before he can demand
        Payment, the buyer pays.

To one he gives a key
With worn-down teeth; to another, braids of hair.
A boy receives *The Book of Common Prayer.*
    Black walnut husks, a diary,
Rooibos tisane. A stuffed blue jay. Bloodstone.
One woman gets a charcoal sketch of her own face,
    And a beautiful girl accepts a carefully sewn
        Pear-scented pillowcase.

The villagers are through.
The swart, kyphotic gravitas-monger swings

To face you. "Think you've understood these things?"
He asks. "Come closer." So you do.
He grabs your hand, brushes your wrist, commands you
To put away your purse. "You'll pay me, by and by,"
He says. He grins. He reaches out and hands you
A damselfly-blue glass eye.

The Reclamation of Paradise

The butterflies' abrupt communiqué
    Said all there was to say.
They would no longer serve as go-betweens
    Or act behind the scenes
On our behalf; no stakeouts, hits, or raids.
    Palm-dappled everglades
Would stay unmapped, the beehives' inner rooms
    Would hum untapped, and blooms
Of ageratum, goldenrod, and clover
    Were *theirs* now. It was over.
We thought we'd had it all impeccably planned;
    We could not understand
This metamorphosis, could not dissect
    Their reasons to reject
Our glorious subversion, so we took
    A long, hard look
At what we needed to succeed again—
    Intelligence—and then
We started out where all those leads begin:
    The net. The jar. The pin.

II. Sidewalk Chalk

In the days that followed children were always screaming.
You could set their hair on fire and, sure enough,
they'd start screaming.

—James Tate

After Grief

You're certain you've been hit but keep on running.
The pine trees' shadows stretch like iron bars.
You feel dizzy and know you'll need your cunning
To find fresh water and navigate by stars.

Before night knits its blanket, you decide
To check the wound. You crouch behind a rock.
The opening is small; the blood has dried.
You pry the bullet out. It starts to talk.

Twenty-First-Century Prothalamion

Because my parents had successful genes
And read the proper toddler magazines,
I won cross-country races in my teens.

Because police patrolled my neighborhood,
Driving the potheads out, I understood
And could respect the need for moral good.

I read deep books in college, studied quarks
And Caravaggio's violent lights and darks,
And kissed your neck one evening as the sparks

Flew upward from a bonfire and starred the air.
I leaned against you, smelled your wood-smoked hair
And held your hand, and knew why I was there:

Amino acids, habit, data. Fate.
I also felt the need to procreate.
That night I chose you, love, to be my mate.

Temptation

You haven't been detected. Nothing breaks
The jungle's muggy silence but the shrug
Of branches where a silvery gibbon makes
A flabbergasting leap. You kneel and tug
The laces of your boots. You're well prepared—
So far, so good. No trip-wire deadfall traps
Have dropped to crush your skull; you can't be snared.
With your next step, the ground beneath you snaps

Open, exposing poison-tipped bamboo
Pikes in a pit. Why would they need a guard?
They knew you'd come to this. *What perfect fakes.*
Their tra-la-la concealed a trou-de-loup,
And you—bamboozled, duped—you take it hard,
As only now you realize the stakes.

Organic Decomposition

Black acts, you blossom from my heart like larkspur
Rotting to pieces while more quickly spreading
To healthy plots. Your rhizomes, firmly threading
Themselves through vertebrae, appear a dark blur
On x-rays: ominous, diffuse. In me
They start the curled ascent to fertile brains,
A garden where they make their ministry
Eradicating all divine remains.

I *wish* my sin were that autonomous,
A parasite or infestation clearing
My name. These shifty metaphors provide
Nothing but distance, artistry veneering
The single blame with doubleness to hide
Intentions hardly so dichotomous.

An Anatomy of Autonomy

If I quench thee, thou flaming minister,
I can again thy former light restore,
Should I repent me . . .

—Othello, *V.ii*

Blue crabs have the ability to sacrifice limbs (called autotomy)
in order to avoid capture. Missing limbs are regrown by a process
called regeneration.

Bitter Crab Disease (BCD) is caused by a blood parasite,
Hematodinium perezi, *a type of dinoflagellate.*

—*www.bluecrab.info*

Let us now praise
This sidling emblem of
The circummotive ways
We walk in love:

When peril prods
It nearer to dismay,
Its blurred pereiopods
Carry away

The crab, whose guard
Commences with its gait,
A side step not too hard
To imitate.

Observe it hide
The tender commonplace
Of its sweet flesh inside
A carapace,

Or show its dread
Of being firmly gripped
By lifting a cheliped
    And brilliant-tipped

Chela, or halt
Intrepid predators
With an abrupt assault;
    The crab prefers

Its privacy,
And will not be constrained.
Sometimes we like to be
    Likewise unchained.

They're not all ex-
ecrable links: sooks mate
Just once, suggesting sex
    Is worth the wait

(The same cannot
Be said for jimmies, who
Without a seemly thought
    Do whom they do),

And in most cases
Their mating cycles boast
Precopulatory embraces
    (As well as post-);

One might concede
During their lusty struggle

Even crustaceans need
   A decent snuggle,

   Which would imply
The worth of a caress
Did crabs not also die
   Of bitterness.

   The crab's inim-
itable in one skill:
If seized by any limb,
   A caught crab will—

   Rather than lose
Its prized autonomy—
Inevitably choose
   Autotomy,

   And make a break
For freedom, so to speak.
So much for freedom's sake.
   But this technique

   We always leave to
The crab, and with good cause:
We much prefer to cleave to
   Love by the claws.

Message on a Bottle

We'd chosen to invest
Cash in advance because we were distressed
By signs we saw implying
We lacked a certain something: *cancer rates*
And military states
Are rising; the dollar's weak; we're still denying
The current atmosphere
Is thinning daily; not much else is clear.
Since we were all relying
On breakthroughs from the pharmacologist,
Now we're good and pissed
That trials have not been wholly satisfying:
Side effects include
Tremors, sweats, nausea, sudden shifts in mood,
The shits, and fits of crying.
The fine print on the bottle cap chimes in,
One in ten players will win,
But you are one of nine, so thanks for trying!
Your dust is only dust,
Your countermeasures bust, and living just
The slowest form of dying.

Not at the Grave of Dylan Thomas

The rows of gravestones jut
   Up from the grass like graying teeth,
A half-jaw smile in no sense undercut
    By the bodies underneath
Lost in the many poses of repose
    By which death mocks
Their hold on life. Behold the remnants: rose,
Smutched shovel, and a lately buried box.

   Who am I kidding? Here
    I am, engrossed by all the gory
Particulars, proclaiming them austere
    But fierce memento mori,
When really all these forceful lamentations
    Seem a bit forced.
Woe to the bones and their disintegrations,
Woe to the veins through which warm blood once coursed,

   Woe to the woeful skin,
    Woe to the whole bewoed shebang!
Honestly. How did we get taken in
    By letting it all hang
Out, as if authenticity depended
    On histrionics,
As if a graveyard couldn't be transcended
With a few blunts or a few gin and tonics?

   Besides, as mentioned, I'm
    Not at the grave of Dylan Thomas,

And I don't care about childhood, grief, time,
    Rage, or excessive commas.
I hate prophetic poets; they are wrong.
    They ought to call
A spade a spade, stop stringing us along.
Death does, indeed, have dominion over all.

Lines for an Inspirational Poster

Shoot for the moon, for even if you miss,
You'll land amongst the stars. Hardly the case.
The more precise conclusion would be this:
You miss, you die, cold and alone in space.

III. Elegies and Valedictions

. . . the music at the quarky heart of things is elegiac.

—Albert Goldbarth

Upon First Viewing *Ball of Fire*

Oh, Barbara Stanwyck, strike
My fancy, stoke my fire,
With one fell stroke revoke my self-control —
Come be the dancing mistress of my soul!
I'll never meet your like
Now that most flicks require
Two topless shots for every minor role;
You couched your sex appeal
In what you could conceal,

A trick that wildly trumps
Modern celebutantes'.
Your smirk and three dry words could flood a room
With oomph! with awww! with va-va-voom!,
To quote those forties chumps.
I guess a real man wants
The panoramic rack and nipple-zoom;
I want the wit, the verve,
And every subtle curve

Of your elaborate con-
versation. Steal my heart,
Toy with it, torch it; mesmerize me; come,
Your slim hips swinging like a pendulum;
And once — no, now — you've gone,
Let me play Krupa's part,
Tapping "Drum Boogie" on a matchbox-drum
With (greatest of his tricks)
A pair of matchstick-sticks.

Soul

i.m. Ray Charles, June 10, 2004

I

Brother Ray, if heaven exists, I hope that
God's prepared a suitably grand piano,
One that proves you've always deserved the pearly
    Keys of the kingdom.

Here, what little comforts we're left with: albums,
Concert footage, snapshots and satyr stories—
Godforsaken keepsakes that hardly help us
    Stave off our grieving

When we hear your voice on an old recording
Crooning blues or climbing the staves to heaven,
Hear the trills and shimmering rolls you played to
    Flesh out a measure,

Hear you laugh mid-verse, and remember nothing
Else will break your permanent earthly silence.
Not that I would downplay your purring vocals'
    Visceral power—

Modern Sounds in Country and Western Music
Oozes sweet, raw soul—but I know their limits;
Once you died, not even your songs could bring you
    Back to your body

Of devoted fans. In a twinkling, trumpets
Stopped their smooth accompaniment and cymbals
Ceased to splash. The worst of it was we always
      Knew we would lose you.

      II

Some dumb preachers labeled it "devil's music."
What would I have done to defend your calling?
Pitch a fit? For harmony's sake, keep silent?
      Turn to the Bible's

Sexy parts? Attempt to explain your plaintive
Love songs sprang from something devout inside you?
Each flung scruple stung like a stone of judgment;
      Pebble by pebble,

True to crow and pitcher, you filled with something.
Call them *whetstones*: all of them made you keener,
Sharpening your ears till you heard the music
      Coming together—

Church and sex as bedfellows, hallelujah
Chords and rakish play-with-your-poodle lyrics
Coupled in a stroke of concerted genius.
      Welcome to stardom.

Now I sit in darkness and play your records—
"Hard Times," "Cry," "You Won't Let Me Go"—and try to
Sound out through these melodies something only
      Music can tell me.

Mostly I remember your favorite gesture:
Singing to the crowd, you would hug yourself in
Joyful grief and testify that without her
    Love, you were nothing.

III

Promise me that God will accept the faithless
Husbands, heartless fathers, and double-dealers.
Promise me that God in his heart has room for
    Heroin addicts,

Alcoholics, ass-grabbing creeps, and bastards,
Not because I want to accuse you, Ray Charles
(Even though you suckered for junk, you also
    Beat it in rehab;

Even though you browbeat your best musicians,
Every note was gold), but because I'm certain
All those freaks and miscreants find safe refuge
    Somewhere inside me.

Brother Ray, remind me that Jesus made you
Keys of pearl and strings of the finest substance
Ever known, that now you compose and play pitch-
    Perfect arrangements;

Tell me how the riffs you let rip on earth are
Nothing next to heavenly scales, how music
Sounds to someone who is at last no longer
    Paying the piper;

Tell me, Brother Ray, how the smallest details
Matter, how eternal fermata ring out,
How the blessed, celestial chanters sing in
        Praise of the grace notes.

Upon Finishing Don Juan

His speech was a fine sample, on the whole,
Of rhetoric, which the learn'd call "rigmarole."

—Byron

But Byron, and Bryon's poetry, never forgets for very long the
provisional and rhetorical character of what he and it are doing.

—Jerome McGann

Your book's cracked spine's white creases
Compose an inverse bar code that, when scanned,
Registers how a reader's bliss increases
    The less he needs well-planned
Excursions into Nature eisegesis
And can instead accept as bona fide
    Your priceless wit's caprices;
And I, who've joined the club, take them in stride,
Dig the digressions in your diegesis.
    Your masterpiece was panned
On moral grounds; and true, you lacked phronesis
From time to time—I'll never understand
    Your grasp of love ("It's me, sis!
You free tonight?"), and even friends decried
Your cantos' frequent, blatant anamnesis—
    But since you've been denied
The chance to pen your last epexegesis,
Your epic—Bloomed, Fryed, Bated, and McGanned—
    Has had to rest in pieces,
The final, partial witness to your grand
Apotheosis, aposiopesis.

Elegy for Paul deLay

I

It might begin with liquid silver trills,
    A scintillant, chromatic
Effusion of upper-octave notes that fills
    The soundscape; an emphatic
Rhythmic torque sets it spinning, and it spills

Into the mellow middle register
    Where you begin to draw
Thick minor sixths that sound like tearing paper—
    Harmonica as raw
As homemade rotgut—before the mercurial blur

Of jazz-inflected patterns, spiraling thirds
    And tritone leaps that show
Your skill in weaving disparate musical threads.
    Your solo, oh-so-low
Now, dirty as ditchwater, starts its slow

Burn back to the top, tripping over bar
    After bar of blues,
Scaling the smoky phrases; and you are
    The spark that gnaws the fuse,
The crackling light, the fallen, rising star

Intent on tightwire walking to the top
    On pure melodic conjecture

In cosmic modes, combining grace and grit
   Until you drop and hit
Your signature sandpaper-rough double stop.

II

What no one else would know
Is that I called you once.

I'd e-mailed you some questions,
Asking for harp advice;
I never dreamt that link
Would let me hear your voice,
But Peter Dammann sent
Your number and a note—
Paul isn't digital yet;
Why don't you give him a call?—
And when I did, we spent
A half hour on the phone.
Me: small-town college kid;
You: world-class blues harp ace.
You didn't need to find
The time for me, but did.

You mentioned third position
Was mostly unexplored,
Said you tongue-blocked the top
Four holes, and underscored
How Little Walter punched
His blow notes; every tip

Has proven nice and strong.
I wrote them down. And look,
I never did erase
You from my address book.
I still can hear your voice —
Heartbreaking, brokenhearted,
Infusing every song
With grief since you've departed.

I didn't know you would
Be gone so soon, so long.

III

Who'd try to play it off as not the least
    Ironic that your last
Album was live? It gives you at your best:
    Now bragging that you left her,
Now breaking down, now backfiring into laughter —
    The heart's whole range compressed
Into an hour-long recording. We were blessed.

The album ending, having cast your spell,
    You finish with a spiel
About the band and introduce them all.
    You say, *We had such fun.*
We'd love to come back, do another one.
    I hear the audience call,
We'd like that, too. We'd like that. Come back, Paul.

Dracula *in Spanish: Imitations of Immortality*

I've just discovered *Dracula* in Spanish.
Not a dubbed version of the black and white
Bela Lugosi starred in, but a separate take.
 It turns out that at night,
 After the English-speaking cast would vanish,
 Hispanic actors would revamp the script,
 Use the same castle, parlor, yard, and crypt,
  And try to top the English cast.
  Mostly they longed to make
A version of the movie that would last.

It's spookier, it's sexier—it's spectacular.
Renfield, attacked in Transylvania by
Dracula's wives, succumbs on-screen (in '31!)
 As later he will die
 Strangled on-screen, the scene so cold, so—Dracular?—
 I shiver when he's throttled and then thrown
 Down for the count; and watching it alone,
  I almost hear old movie reels
  During the first night's run,
Turning and turning on their silver wheels.

The costumes differ: Helen Chandler wears
These scarf-and-pleat ensembles as risqué
As cotton tablecloths; her wardrobe pales beside
  The black silk negligee
 Carmen Guerrero sleeps in and which bares
 So much—shucks, most of her!—that I lament
 Her minor part as the impertinent

Best friend who meets the Count, is smitten,
    And all too soon has died
In bed, sheet-white, forever shy once bitten.

    Well, not that shy. She chomps some children later
    And shambles through a foggy graveyard shot
Because she, too, is now a vampire; and her function,
        To aggravate the plot
    As one of Dracula's dead brides. No greater
    Love than immortal love, right? More than all
Her sexy stays and stalkings, I'll recall
        What English-version viewers miss
        Due to undue compunction:
Her punctured throat, the fangs behind the kiss.

    I love the sidemen — Barry Norton's Harker
    Purrs suave concern and looks much handsomer;
Van Helsing's quirky brows, huge nose, and goofy ears
        Are perfect — but prefer
    Lugosi's Dracula: a smoother, starker
    Manifestation of the morbid drive
To stay, no matter what he kills, alive.
        Faced with a mirror's clear exposure,
        Lugosi strikes it, sneers,
And willfully regains his self-composure

    In seconds; but *el Conde* smashes it
    Almost cartoonishly. When *he* confronts
Van Helsing, both prolong the tension they contrive;
        Lugosi all at once
    Hisses and rushes forward, his eyes lit
    With dark, primeval hatred. Faced with this,
I realize how little artifice

Is needed to portray such pure
      Evil as is alive
Within us—careful, patient, without cure.

Sometimes I fear what will survive of us
Are countless permutations of that face;
Whatever species we become will recognize
      The depth of our disgrace
In all the photos where that furious
Grimace earmarks a soldier ruined for good
Or lurks beneath a Ku Klux Klansman's hood.
      Perhaps our distant progeny
         Will say of our demise,
Death had become the final remedy.

Enough of metaphysics. One bier downed,
The Count has vowed to confer the vampire's curse
On Eva—leading lady dealt a deuce—and damn her
      Forever to rehearse
Bloodcurdling acts, then lay low underground.
Here let us pity Helen Chandler's fate—
To all alone beweep her outcast state—
      Since you, dear Eva, steal the show;
         One glimmer of your glamour
Makes sober Helen one more so-and-so.

Why do I love you? Let me count the whys:
Your honey-tinctured voice, your turns of phrase—
The night enchants me and *may all your dreams be red*—
      Your shudders and sashays,
And maybe most of all for how your eyes
Look crazy when you bite your boyfriend's neck—

Again, on-screen. No innocent little peck,
　　No friendly hookup hickey there!
　　　　As Mrs. Browning said,
Love snags and drags us backward by the hair.

The climax? Come on, friends, plot spoilers stink;
Besides, it's boilerplate. For closure's sake,
Let's say that Dracula's ultimate loss of Eva's soul
　　　　Turns on the grave mistake
　　Of spurning mortal love, which cannot sink
　　To nothingness like fame but must outlast
　　The corpora of knowledge, art, the cast—
　　　　Except, dear Eva, all that said,
　　　　　　In your immortal role
You'll always be my Queen of the Undead.

IV. Voices in My Head

For I hear many whispering . . .

—Jeremiah 20:10

The Therapist on Teleology

Excellent question, one for which there is
No simple answer. After eighteen years
Of practice, I've had no two people give
The same account of what it is they want.
One man so patiently explained his life
Would have been better with a bigger penis,
I half agreed with him; another said
He loved his wife, his car, his kids, his job,
But wished his microwave would quiet down—
It kept intoning prophecies and then
Proclaiming them fulfilled in thirty seconds.
In any case, your question brings me back
To early in my practice when a woman,
A secretary, sought me out because
She was afraid. We met for several months.
During our first appointment, she described
The new compulsion that had frightened her:
In the few weeks before she'd come to me,
Whenever she would see a colleague shred
Pieces of paper—notes or old reports,
Receipts or minor confidential files—
She'd wait until the colleague left and then
Race to the trash can, where she would begin
To rifle through it, searching for the scraps.
She'd gather them, as many as she could,
And take them home; there she would reconstruct
Whatever document or note it was,
Taping the pieces to her dinner table.

Most of it was predictably inane
(Memos that needed no response, a temp's
"I'm bored, I'm bored, I'm bored" penned twenty times
Across the backs of envelopes), but sometimes,
Scattered among the salvaged grocery lists
And scrawled reminders to delouse the dog,
She'd find a private message—dates for trysts,
Fraudulent trusts, that sort of thing—and once,
A short handwritten letter: *Harriet,*
Forgive me. You should take him back. Love, Frank.
I asked her what she thought of when she read
Her compilation. "Nothingness," she said.
"Its grammar, its morphology, its meaning."
She had a way with words. Before she stopped
Scheduling sessions, she described her table.
"Doctor, the surface has become uneven.
Layers of tape and paper have transformed it
Into a motley topographic map
Of secrecy and grief. I run my fingers
Over the ridges and I realize
That every vestige of significance
Will vanish." She had such a way with words.
I ask you, what did *she* want? Evidence
For blackmail? Gossip for her friends? Control?
Or just coherence, something to resist
The dissolutive train of entropy?
I still can't tell you. Nonetheless, I think
Of her disorder—even there the term
Belies itself—and wonder if she might have
Believed there was a single slip of paper,
A message, maybe just one word, that would
Justify all that searching to herself;

And I can picture her across from me,
Nervously shredding a tissue in her hands,
Then cupping and recupping it until
It looked for all the world like a white carnation.

Being Undressed

The older girl next door
Has left his T-shirt hummocked on the floor,
And he has never felt
Such tremors as her fingers at his belt—
He's certain now he's caught
Her lunchtime stares, her clinking forks of thought—
But when his mother knocks,
The neighbor girl collects her sky-blue socks,
Kicks out the window screen,
And wriggles through. What happened there between
Them (almost) dissipates
More quickly than he'd wish, although he waits
An extra second after
He hears the broken china of her laughter.

Masterpiece Interrupted by Hobo, Park Bench, 1999

First lines are tough. Let's see . . . *The red horizon*
—Scratch that. Red: passion, rage—too sentimental.
The APRICOT *horizon near Marseilles*
Blossomed briefly, and then began to wither.
I felt time loosen. The tree leaves lisped ça marche *in*
Regretful French, and their imperfect sigh lent

A wooden weight—or should the trees be silent?
Is this too much "gaze toward the drear horizon"
Drivel? More academic, then: *When Marcian*
Summoned the Council, the note he sent—a mental
Note to self: find the note—*asked bishops whether*
Jesus was human or divine and—
                              "Mars, eh?"

A hobo eyes my sheet. "Name's Omar. Say,
You got a light?" I glare at him, am silent;
If glares were pesticide, this clod would wither.
"A cigarette?" I gaze toward the horizon
And am unaffected by this sentimental
Stereotype of poor—
                    "*I* seen a Martian

One night while I was driving past a marsh in
Northeastern Florida. Crashed my truck."
                              "Marseilles,"
I start to say to instill a sentiment—
                              "All
Hell done broke loose! At first, my wife was silent,

But when them bright lights almost done her eyes in,
She started screaming. Fog rolled up, the weather

All wonky—see my thumb? They made it wither.
Hot damn, no! Never want to see a Martian.
Needed a cell phone—what's their name? Horizon?"
To him, I say, "Verizon"; to Marseilles,
The sunset, trees, and Marcian, I mouth a silent
Adieu. Perhaps I'm just a sentimental

Poet who struggles under a sentimental
Model of composition, smitten with—
                                        "Er,
You listening, buddy? You been awful silent."

My eyes drop. Bleeding cut on Omar's shin,
Split sides on Omar's shoes. Could Omar say
Anything now that would not be hair-raising?

I think of water, robes, a choir raising
Voices as priests march in. I think of silence,
The only mercy not too sentimental.

The Nickname

So, after being gut-punched, groin-kicked, dragged by my hair
down a gravel drive and left near an empty mailbox
by love, which has a knack for this, I end up watching
Invasion of the Body Snatchers, eating too much
Number Five (beef with peapods) from the Greedy Dragon,
and really regretting my decision to pair this
particular meal with this particular movie
since the movie's extraterrestrial clones hatch from
huge pods that look like bigger versions of my dinner.
Also, the protagonists are recently divorced.
Still, you've got to admire how the pods shudder and froth
and spit out waxy replicas of their victims, who
stand, axes in hand, ready to hack themselves apart.

I love these classic films, but that's part of what makes me
an "old soul," as my high school English teacher put it.
When I imagine how my real life should have gone, it
always resembles an Agatha Christie novel.
You know, rural England, the 1920s, I am
a vicar or a village constable and I tend
a backyard garden—foxglove, forget-me-nots, sweet peas—
and I may or may not do some amateur sleuthing,
depending on (a) whether I am an amateur,
which of course I would not be were I the constable,
and (b) whether there are murders there, which seems to be
related to the number of sleuths in a village—
if Miss Marple ever croaks, local crime will plummet!

After my taste grew more sophisticated, I got
rid of most of my Agatha Christie books; I kept
And Then There Were None, though, which I guess was ironic.
I have always had fairly discriminating taste—
I was that one kid who could drink with a blindfold on
and tell you whether it was Pepsi, RC, or Coke—
but that doesn't mean I didn't have plenty to learn;
I had a Jane Austen teacher in college who said,
"The most important distinction between characters
is some are educable, some ineducable."
Chalk up Dr. Bennell, the hero of *Invasion*,
to the latter category—a third of the way
through the movie, and he still hasn't gotten a thing.

Anyway, these townspeople appear to have no souls,
it's great! I'm pretty sure I've met my fair share of those!
I have a code name for them: I call them the Fish Eyes.
You know, the glassy stares, the gaping mouths . . . My parents
used to tell me: "Mark, what's stupid is picking others
apart." I guess the pod-people aren't dumb, they just lack
emotions; still, you'd think Dr. Bennell would see through
the psycho-mumbo-jumbo the local shrink uses
to explain the weird "You're not my mom!" phenomenon
overtaking the town: the shrink jabbers on about
mass hallucinations and hysteria, which is
funny because hysteria derives from the Greek
word *hysterikós*, meaning "suffering in the womb"—

you see what I mean? It all comes down to girl problems.
These flat expressions and monotonic monologues
probably just mean that everybody in town got
run over by the dump truck of love. Well, not really.

Also, "suffering in the womb" does not equal "girl
problems." But you've got to admire the linguistic flair,
the tongue-in-cheekery of it, right? Call it a gift.
Once in my middle school Latin class a kid I knew
sneezed so hard he broke all the blood vessels in his eye,
leaving it a bright, wet red very hard to look at,
so I called him "Shoculus" for the rest of the year,
a sobriquet of which I'm particularly proud.
Anyway, Dr. B kisses the leading lady,

and she says, "It happened, Jack, I fell asleep," and then
she's one of them, a soulless automaton bent on
his being vegetally replaced in kind, and now
I think, "Ooh, ooh, they're tellin' my story! They're tellin'
my *story!*"—yep, me and the Doc are as like as two
bees in a swarm—except then Doc drops her in the mud
and starts hauling butt, and I think, "Hmmm, definitely
not my story anymore," since I can see myself
still glubbing in that mud puddle, trying to argue
with what's-her-face that she has not in fact gone to sleep,
that we are all still in love and me and her and her
hysterical womb are going to have fantastic
lives together, and not fantastic in the sense of

"belonging or pertaining to fantasy," but in
the *boom-chickita-kaaahhh* sense of Yello's hit, "Oh Yeah"—
beautiful and more beautiful, with luxurious
desserts and oodles of sex. Still, Doc's probably right—
love 'em and leave 'em once they morph into pod-bred fiends
who want to peel away your rich emotional life.
Of course, none of this helps a thing when I start to think
about my latest girlfriend, how I used to kiss her

uncritically on her neck, how we had a scrapbook
about a third full of pictures with haiku captions—

   Blue-eyed girl with hand
   of boyfriend. Shame on him, hid
   just outside the frame!

                    —or how before we started to snap
at each other all the time and for no good reason,

she used to call me Snow Pea, and then sometimes just Snow.

Reading Pilgrim's Progress While Waiting to Be Tested for STDs

As *Faithful* blabbers on about his tussle
With *Wanton* (So the clincher was he closed
His eyes? Virtue takes less than I'd supposed . . .),
I glimpse a blur of flesh—bronze skin, taut muscle—

And quickly am embedded in my own
"Inward and carnal cogitations" while
A short skirt's high heels click across the tile
And out the door. I probably should atone

For staring, but a nurse has called my name;
Clipboard in hand, she leads me to a room
To check my temp and pulse while her perfume
Suffuses me in more of the sensual same.

Poor *Faithful* was bedeviled first by lust
And then by *Christian* ("Doctor will be in
Shortly . . . ") inspecting him for venial sin
And saintly vigor while they each discussed

His painful pilgrimage. "What brings you here
Today?" the doctor asks, stepping inside,
Where fact and fable seem to coincide.
"A test for syphilis?" I must appear

As baffled as I feel because he adds,
"For gonorrhea? Herpes? HIV?"

I need to be specific? "Better be
Safe, test for everything. You undergrads

Are shameless." Then he smiles. "A urine sample,
We'll draw some blood, and you'll be free to go."
So all young men are undergrads? "I know
You don't want lectures, but here is an example

Of what can happen to an oversexed,
Underprotected male. Take this brochure."
Blisters and itching, burning piss, *no cure*,
But I am thinking of my Bunyan text—

The first eight paragraphs, to be exact—
And am afraid. The doctor's read me wrong;
The delectation (e.g., stare too long)
Is not consent (i.e., the fucking fact),

And I am getting tested not because
I am promiscuous (I've only had
Two partners, both monogamous—not bad
For one whose earliest Madonna was

A pop star armored in bizarre brassieres),
But to assure my girlfriend we will be
Safe in the refuge of our intimacy.
I picture *Christian*'s fingers in his ears,

Fleeing the ruined city ("Now, with AIDS . . . "),
Abandoning his children and his wife
And crying out, "Life! Life! Eternal life!"
(" . . . worldwide . . . "), apocalyptic cavalcades

There at his back, and now it seems absurd
To listen to this lecture on diseases
When wrestling with a God whom no one pleases,
The same one ("Any questions?") who preferred

His own son's death before a single child
Should live estranged from him. What will he not
Demand that I give up since he once fought
With love itself to leave us reconciled?

When high-toned glossy shots or neophytes
Decide which sinners merit God's abhorrence,
They always pick the gonorrheal Gomorrans
And sybaritic, syphilitic Sodomites,

And when they figure which ones should receive
The silver ribbons or the golden bowls,
They pick themselves, claiming their purchased souls
As proof of their admission. They believe

("I'll see you out . . . ") that no one can dispute
Schemes of supernal rights and carnal wrongs.
(Does anyone still read *The Song of Songs*?)
Mine is a vision far more absolute:

That God has given so much for our sake
To see us ("Through that door there . . . ") face to face
That he is indiscriminate with grace,
And there is nothing that he will not take.

V. Absence Makes the Heart

As discourse about God cannot teach us about God,
so discourse about love cannot teach us about love.

—H. L. Hix

XOXOXO

Let the more loving one be me.

—Auden

She brings her ten-page letters to a close
With stylish *x*'s and expressive *o*'s
In little lines, like stitches, to impart
Her sense of their infrangible connection;
On his he draws a tin-can phone and heart,
His tangible conceit for their affection.

They send each other seasonal bouquets,
Boxes of truffles, lemongrass sachets.
They track months' passage with a felt-tip marker
And joke that Time is warring with the sexes.
If day by day their calendars grow darker
And boxed-in weeks become a row of *x*'s,

They seem to have decided that these scraps
Of crisscrossed paper are the treasure maps
For Once-Upon-A-Time and Long-Ago;
Still cross-eyed drunk with love, they must confuse
Their hugs-and-kisses game of tic-tac-toe
With something that the two of them can't lose.

Patience

She thanks him for his patience, and he pauses
Over the probably subconscious causes

That she, so distant, chose this word to deal
A compliment to him. She says she'll feel

Much better once she's home, but all he's heard
Is the explosion of that loaded word:

It smolders like a single diamond set
In an engagement ring. He can't forget—

Although by now perhaps he shouldn't care—
That patience is a name for solitaire.

Streetlight and Stars

I stood there on the balcony with nothing
On but a pair of boxers. Streetlights hung
    An awkward, orange haze
Over the dingy pavement while the air
Reverberated with the city's murmurs—
Terse car-horn honks of Morse code gibberish,
    Rap lyrics, thudding bass lines,
The pops and crystalline burbles of breaking glass.

I'd almost just made love. We'd opted not to.
My girlfriend joined me on the balcony,
    Dressed in her bra and panties;
We stood there side by side, not saying much
Until she offered, "The other day I read
This crazy article that claimed the stars
    Spelled out the gospel message—
Leo and Virgo stood for Christ and Mary."

I think she wanted to connect with me
Because we'd stopped. "That's kind of weird," I said.
    "I thought so, too," she said,
Recoiling from the sound of squealing tires
A few blocks down. "You just can't trust the Web."
We watched the moon, as clear-edged as the moon
    In movies where they use
A blue screen to create a starry background.

I thought about how planets, "wanderers"
In Greek, moved backward through the sky

And caused the complications
That plagued the Ptolemaic universe—
Elaborate epicycles, deferents,
And equant points that made a king remark,
    "Had God consulted me,
I would have recommended something simpler."

I kind of missed that old cosmology
With Earth dead center, all those perfect circles,
    The *Primum Mobile,*
And that celestial music Dante heard
When he first started hurtling toward the stars,
Drawn by a love that seven hundred years
    Ago could leave him weightless,
Immune to gravity. All things considered,

Maybe I should have tried a little harder
To talk to her: maybe I should have told her
    I suddenly respected
The sheer lucidity of our desire
Or that I longed for the empyrean.
Before I could, she shivered, went inside,
    And started getting dressed.
"You should come in. I'll try to find that link,"

She said, her voice a little flat. I waited
A few more minutes, though, despite the cold,
    Enamored of my thoughts,
And through the sliding door I watched as her
Computer screen blinked to a vibrant blue
And white block letters spelled out SYSTEM FAILURE.
    I didn't go back in
Until a streetlight flickered and went out.

Nocturne in the Key of Water

As the last chord softens the symphony
    Into a manageable hum,
Muting the memory of the tympani
With slurred adieus from horns and clarinets
    Until the orchestra goes dumb
      And everyone regrets

The silence porous with an awkward cough
    And gentle banter, so our few
Last words resolved before your moving off
And ceding me to silence. I have grown
    Accustomed to rooms without you,
      Am comfortably alone.

From my front porch, I have a front-row seat
    As virtuoso thunderstorms,
Stirred by an audience so incomplete,
Compose their atmospheric movements for
    The empty house, and insect swarms
      Cling to the closed screen door.

The pizzicato raindrops lave the street
    And lace the evening air with taps
Like fingertips on glass while I retreat
To recollections of the night we met;
    As my mind turns, the thunderclaps
      Applaud its pirouette.

From what I can recall, I can't believe
    I've let you go: your repartees
Could score me like these lightning bolts that weave
With phosphorescent spiderwebs of light
        The temporary tapestries
            Unraveling me tonight,

And no one else could do that. You've become
    The pattern of these brilliant lines,
The minor melody I sometimes hum
When contrapuntal lightning scars the sky
        And running rainwater defines
            All that it is to be dry.

Just let me lean into this water's song,
        Dip closer to the sable pool
And feel its subtle pull lead me along
As Hylas felt her fingers, interlaced,
        On the small of his back, and felt her cool,
            Strong arms surround his waist.

Domestic Operetta for One Voice

I

aria con coloratura

Beyond this empty room, the empty house
    Offers condolences.
A faucet drips its intermittent tears;
The furnace stutters, stunned; the glassware stares;
    The fridge retreats to silence. Is
Nothing intact? Outside, a wound-up hose
Gargles its sudden grief, the hollyhocks
Stand openmouthed, and sputters of sorrow cascade
From a scrapped engine that the neighbor kid
    Patiently chokes.

Forgive me, love, if all this grief appears
    A little overwrought;
Somehow I always find it in these empty
Rooms—this anonymous farce of empathy,
    Worse than the worst I ever wrote—
A poltergeist or haint. This house conspires
Against me, every bit from grout to grating.
The wall-cracks speak, the peeling paint complains.
We both know theirs are not the only lines
    That I'm regretting.

So I immerse myself in mindless chores:
    Vacuum five times a week,
Empty the trash in every room once daily,

Scour the shower. If I lie here idly
   Thinking, my thoughts keep me awake
Until I start up odd jobs at odd hours,
Like last night: washing dishes, wishing, dreaming,
I let hot water run so long it scalded
My hands. You would have kissed me, pointed, scolded,
   Our glasses steaming.

   II

             monodic reprise

Another Friday night.
Strata of dirty plates,
Outcrops of opaque cups,
And, yes, the kitchen sink.

Plenty of time to think.

I stop the drain and twist
The scummed hot water knob,
Start throwing in the dishes.
Amidst the mess, I note

How little a man keeps

After the all-out screaming:
Gone are the crystal stems;
Gone, the heirloom silver.
Now in the crumb-filled drawers

I catch a glimpse of silver-

fish flashing umber backs
Before they disappear;
Now in the sudsy water
Plastic utensils bob

Like drowning mariners,

And I rinse out cheap glasses
So fragile that at times
One shatters in my fist—
In this, my empty empire,

The least of many losses.

I wish the hardwood floors
Presaged a better future,
But every single feature,
From red wine stains and cracks

To waxy sheens, inures

Me to the facts: my wishes
The days alone have trampled;
Ditto the nights, my dreams.
I stand here washing dishes,

My flannel shirtfront rumpled,

And know that nothing sweeter
Looms in the air, no kinder
Version of life awaits
Me, so I slip my hand in

The angry sink, abandon

Caution and feel the water
Scalding my skin. (No won-
der that at this point when
I set it on the counter,

The glass keeps steaming.)

III

sotto voce

The tepid water ripples in the sink,
Then settles, smooth and gray as dirt-grimed glass.
I never needed you. These evenings pass;
So will the oddness of my solitude.
      I read, I write, I think
About *Persuasion*. Thoughts of you intrude.

I've run the gamut from gemütlichkeit
To spite, and nothing works. I can't ignore
The frigid gusts breathing across the floor
(Ghostly enjoinders not to walk alone),
      The bedsprings' overbite,
Or the late traffic's faint, bathetic drone.

Sometimes I dream you'll make it back to me:
I'll hear your tires crunch in the gravel drive,
You'll sing how grand it is to be alive,
And, à la fifties scripts, we'll start the weeping-
      And-kissing jubilee;
But when I dream those dreams, I'm rarely sleeping.

Sleep is too honest an activity
For those scenarios and their reprieve
From waking life; in all real dreams, you leave.
The screen door slams again. The car horn blares.
        I shout, "At last, I'm free!"
And climb the porch's Sisyphean stairs,

Which leaves me here: awake in bed at night,
Trying to map our life's disintegration,
Praying for some last-ditch illumination,
I am (and am no longer) of two minds,
        And all I get of light
Are passing headlights punching through the blinds.

        IV

                grand finale

Look at me, decomposing on the couch —
A grade-A, grand slam, dumb, disgraceful slouch.

I've ditched love, lust, and even innuendo
And now devote myself to my Nintendo,

Whose buttons I can push without concern;
Plus, since I'm flying solo, it's my turn

Whenever I decide it is (which rocks).
I've spent four days in the same pair of socks

And somehow think myself fully equipped
With just two food groups: Fried and Double-Dipped.

I'm getting by. With fewer gasps and thrills,
I'll grant you, and I've found my social skills

Need cleaning up—for everyone I meet,
I've got one cycle: Blather, Wince, Repeat—

But still, I'm getting by. Which is to say,
I miss you, Sara. Pardon that cliché.

I know that nothing I dream up will be
Perfect enough to draw you back to me,

That we have lost our chance at growing old
Together and will never be consoled

By one another's wrinkles, that I am
Unlikely to become your Abraham;

But hear me out. Table that last decision
And see what I see with a kinder vision.

Years have elapsed, and you have called at last.
We have agreed to share a brief repast.

You bring a salad in a wooden bowl
Pitifully dented, scratched, and pocked, but whole;

Its blemishes resemble woodcut rain.
The salad is your specialty: romaine

You surely bought this morning, walnuts, pears,
Raspberry vinaigrette. We scoot our chairs

Closer together. Somehow we've forgiven
Each other everything that would have driven

Us crazy had we tried to make it back
When, grain by grain, the strain began to crack

The hourglass of our love. Would we have lasted?
Who knows? But now we feast where once we fasted,

And I can tell that you have missed this place
By every ghost that plays across your face:

You wonder where our drinking glasses went,
Why the new plates, given the old ones meant

So much to both of us. Gone, my dear. Done.
Over the years I broke them one by one,

Some in the grip of fury, some in grief,
Some from pure klutziness. Is there relief

In knowing parts of me will never change?
Even the meal I've cooked has come out strange,

But we partake of it as if it weren't
A hodgepodge hot dish, part half-baked, part burnt.

And then? Well, just dessert. Our time is waning.
We thank each other for the entertaining

Evening, you grab your purse, you glance at me;
I hear myself blurt, *Would you like some tea?*—

As if our first shy tea dates hadn't led
To making love at daybreak in your bed.

(We must have drunk a thousand cups before
We realized we were becoming more

Than friends, before the red parenthesis
On the cup's edge—your lipstick's half-a-kiss—

Became the understood *of course* to whether
We'd ever always want to be together.)

You sit back down, and from a topmost shelf
I bring out what I'd hidden from myself:

The fragile china cups we used to use
Back in our love-drunk days. I didn't lose

Or break them. No one else has ever sipped
A drop of tea from them. The rims are chipped,

And small gray fissures spread like tiny maps
Of where we might have gone had we perhaps

Had better luck, more patience, fewer words.
Since second looks become diminished thirds,

Suspended fourths, and hollow fifths that fade
Into the separate parts that we have played,

Why take those steps down memory's fractured lines?
I measure out the tea. We'll read the signs—

The tacit, loose leaf patterns in the lees—
Later; for now, there's now. No prophecies.

I pour the water. Sara, let's be clear,
Now that we're near my vision's end, that here—

Wherever *here* is—is where I will be
Should you decide you want this cup of tea;

And I will wait here, as our tea leaves steep,
Content to keep whatever we can keep

Together as our cups release their pair
Of mist-skinned tendrils curling through the air,

Vaporous cracks in the invisible
Wall that divides us, loose threads time will pull,

Sweet incense smoke that means we can redeem
All we have lost in sarabands of steam.

VI. A Little Wind and Smoke

To make the point perhaps more graphically, I have done you no harm if I distinguish between your body and your soul. If I separate your body from your soul, however, I have murdered you.

—R. C. Sproul

Autobiography

There is no beauty left in me.
A gecko scuds behind the blinds.
A concertina whines off-key.
A lariat of smoke unwinds
From the unfiltered cigarette
That some distracted flirt has let
Burn unattended while the band
Blurts its pastiche of zydeco
And sixties' soul. I never planned
To let my sense of beauty go,

But something's snagged in me: I watch
A sour bartender twist a rag
And clear the bar top of spilled scotch;
A box blonde jitter through her bag
For her prescription medicine —
Citalopram or Vicodin? —
Until the reassuring smudge
Of orange bottle has appeared;
Another drunk refuse to budge,
Sloshing more scotch that must be cleared;

And a young girl, with such a thin
Shirt that her green bikini glows
Beneath it, groggily begin
Her fifth or sixth; and I suppose
We've all come here because we think
The music, money, flirt or drink

Will be, if not quite beautiful,
At least a decent overture
To something somewhat comparable;
But I, not drunk, am not so sure.

I gigged in bars like this. I stood
On stage, harmonica in hand,
And choked whatever notes I could
From a cheap, tarnished Marine Band,
The sawtooth texture of its comb
Rough on my tongue; I felt at home
Cascading through long solos, singing
To tipsy crowds and half-full glasses,
Biting off riffs for fills—just bringing
Folks pleasure, even if it passes.

It emptied like an ashtray dumped
Into a trash can. Now I see
All the same half-drunk dancers slumped
Against the walls but cannot see
The amber nimbus that surrounded
Them when the amped-up bass resounded
Through the floorboards, the lead guitar
Teetered on the edge of feedback,
The keyboard player teased the bar
With modal solos that would lead back

Into a chorus and the chords
Resolved like sighs . . . I loved to sing.
Sometimes when I forgot the words
I just kept playing, savoring
The changes, holding one long note

For ten full measures; or I'd quote
Duke's "In a Sentimental Mood"
Or Beethoven's *Fifth Symphony*
To prove the music could include
An incidental melody.

Everything seemed phenomenal;
A genuine world began appearing.
I recognized the beautiful
Lime supernova of an earring
Glinting its brilliant crucifix
Down in the crowd. A booth of six
Hard hats erupted in laughter when
The fattest jumped up, spilled his beer
On his huge crotch, sat down again;
"Bill pissed his pants!" they yelled. A cheer.

(I'm there. *I'm there.* Please teach me how
To stay this time.) The whiskey glows;
Illuminated spirits now
Surmount the bar in vitreous rows
Of hazel, chestnut, cherrywood.
Seconds ago, two servers stood
Counting their tips, but they've unbunched
The scrunchies holding up their hair
And shimmy through the layer of crunched
Peanut shells on the floor. (I'm there

And never want to leave.) The band
Starts in B♭—half jazz, half blues—
And then the front man lifts his hand
And quavers, "Nothing left to lose . . . ";

I want to add a harmony
And somehow stumble on the key.
All that exists now is the song—
Triplets, sextuplets, syncopated
Complaints about who done who wrong
Until the lowdown are elated

And I think, *Praise him with the harp*
And lyre, with drums and tambourines,
Praise him in C and in C#,
Because this earthy music means
I can forget myself tonight
And by that mystic oversight
Begin to sense the presence of
God in this acrid, cinerous bar:
So piercing is his sacred love,
It doesn't matter where we are.

Those evenings do not last. The rest
Dissolve in lovelessness despite
The temporary palimpsest
Of memory. (I haven't quite
Returned yet. Let me linger here
Outside of time. Please. Let me hear
This perfect music just once more
Without the spectral imprecision
Of corporeity, before—)
I miss the beatific vision.

They're cashing out the registers.
Band members wind their cords and store
Their microphones. A drunkard slurs

His indignation and slams the door.
Drained glasses clink a tuneless coda
To whiskey sours and flat lime soda
While thunder clatters through the air.
Perhaps it is the soul that fails
The vision. In the streetlights' glare,
The falling rain resembles nails.

Mirror Image

For now we see in a mirror, darkly; but then face to face . . .

—1 Corinthians 13:12a

The steam drifts up
In cycloid puffs, like thoughts in comic strips,
While water drips
Steadily from the showerhead.
I'm almost done; I cup
My hands and rinse my face. Same dry routine . . .
The water's off. I'm clean.

Breath-like, the steam
Has fogged the bathroom mirror; word by word,
Ghostishly blurred,
Clear lines I drew last night appear
In silvery streaks and seem
To taunt me: *I am with you always.* Right.
But always out of sight.

I see my face
Behind the letters, peeking through each break
In the opaque
Surface, and guess the words endure
Because of some faint trace
Of eccrine sweat, the human salts that slip
From every fingertip;

And suddenly
I'm taken back, my finger outstretched to write
These words last night.
Two paintings flicker into view

In counterpoint to me:
One is *Belshazzar's Feast* by Rembrandt, where
    Out of the lamplit air

        A human hand
Condenses, writes a warning on the wall
        About the fall
    From kingship that we know will come,
        And leaves the king unmanned
By how he's made to wallow in the middle
        Of this incisive riddle;

        The other one
Is Michelangelo's creation scene,
        A cross between
    Sheer joy at God's work and the fear
        That it will not be done:
God's outstretched finger drawn to Adam's, curled,
        Encompasses the world.

        I read somewhere
That those are Adam's inches; for Adam's sake,
        God will not take
    Those final inches back. God knows,
        Then, why I stand and stare
At what I've scribbled. Sacrosanct? Divine?
        The script is always mine.

A *Closer Walk with Thee*

> *. . . But the faith and the love and the hope are all in the waiting.*
>
> —*T. S. Eliot*

Sometimes I'm certain I could waste eternity
    Like this—my eyes closed, palms turned up, adept
At none of these God-given sacred disciplines
    But trying nonetheless, yearning to learn
The ins and outs of listening for the Inner Light.
    Today I'm lost to everything except
The Good Lord's everlasting taciturnity.
    I want to blame this rock-hard bench, the pins
And needles in my rear, a Friend's persistent cough,
    Or my own jadedness (that "everlasting"
When I mean "recent") for the way I've wandered off
    All morning, picking at my sweater sleeve
Instead of seeking Jesus. Why I can't discern
    The spirit's leading, given all I've tried—
The studies, prayers, praise, silence, stillness, vigils, fasting—
    I can't explain, but I am mortified.

               *

    The analogues
Are endless . . . As your birthday nears,
    You wait for the surprise
Party, the cake, the presents; no one comes.
    No Disney, no Six Flags.
No wings, no beer. Not even doughnut crumbs.
    Your sister didn't realize
It was today; your mother disappears.

    You tell your best
Friend that you love her; you propose.

She sits straight back and stares
Several feet above and behind your head.
    You shouldn't have professed
Your love, you know it; now you want to hide.
    She looks up, drinking in the stars,
And hands you back your single scarlet rose.

      Your father dies,
    But not before you both run out
      Of things to say. The last
Weeks in the hospital are silent weeks,
    An antiseptic daze.
It clouds the room, so you take frequent walks.
    He dies while you are gone; you list
The things you wish you'd talked with him about.

*

Are these the silences of God?
One day forgetting you are there?
The stare? Not knowing what to say?
The body's silence or the wheeze

Escaping it before it dies?
O Lord of matter and of spirit,
What merit is there in a Word
That lies unspoken? Give it shape.

*

You hear the hiss and lisp of aspen leaves,
The gritty scrape of paper on a sidewalk,
    But you do not hear the wind itself.

You hear the porch swing thud against the house,
The chain-link fence shiver electric ice,
But you do not hear the wind itself.

You hear the wobble of venetian blinds,
The terse slam of an open bedroom door,
But you do not hear the wind itself.

*

Picture a nighttime scene.
Red and blue lights. Bright yellow CAUTION tape
Surrounding the obscene
Chalked outline of a body now reduced
To nothing but its shape
On asphalt, flat and empty. Angel dust.

A couple walking by
After a marvelous date—both moonstruck, each
The other's alibi—
Will barely notice the barricades or hear
The walkie-talkies screech;
They will make love tonight, that much is clear.

Above it all, the moon,
As pale and lustrous as a milky eye,
Almost appears immune
To these apparent tangents' implications:
It opens in the sky
A rabbit hole through which thin emanations

From somewhere plain and pure
Pour across sandlots where the pedophiles
Touch boys and disappear,

Through parlor windows where a Hold 'Em life-
    Long loser gamely smiles
While playing footsie with the Big Blind's wife,

        Past rusty, padlocked gates
And onto weed-crazed lawns until the light
        Silently infiltrates
Even the bedroom where a nervous teen
        Lies waiting for the white
Flash of her boyfriend's briefs—he can't contain

        His joy at getting lucky
Tonight at last—and through the caterwaul,
        The loverly malarkey,
The sensuous susurrus, you can hear
        That laughing couple call
Each other *dear heart*, as if they'd landed here

        Without the barest notion
Of how abjectly love has been expressed
        Or what would set in motion
The torturous intents capped by "six slugs
        Fired at the victim's chest
After his killers had broken both his legs."

        The just and unjust shine
In all that moonlight, luminous confreres
        Until a curdled line
Of clouds elides the moon before it rains;
        But even once it clears,
The light will finally fade when the moon wanes.

This poor, benighted planet.
Let darkness overtake the bland façades
    Of buildings; to explain it,
Let there ring out invective like Elijah's
    ("The *toilette* of the gods?")
Or scores of sacrilegious elegies;

    But can the blithe corrective
Of telling us the darkened moon is just
    A matter of perspective,
The relative positions of the sun
    And earth. THE TRUTH OR BUST,
The bumper sticker reads. You're busted, son.

    (And then there are those hours
The moon declines through firethorn and cerise,
    And prophets claim their powers
Have turned the moon to blood as holy writ
    Predicted. Now one sees
The shadow of the world has covered it.)

                    *

Oh, come on, everybody's done it once;
    Some people, once per day.
A pale, befuddled friend starts to confide
    One of his beer-brained stunts
To your safekeeping; you, attentive, say,
    "You know, you could have died . . . "

And lo, Great Sage! you're giving him advice:
    You're solemn, witty, wise —
Why, practically the Oracle at Delphi,
    Except you're more precise!

It takes so long for you to realize
　　You're talking to yourself.

　　　　　*

Often the prayer
Begins, *You there?*,
Intensifies
To candid cries
And litanies
Of, *Would you please . . .* ,
Then tapers off
To a wet cough
And a taut gut.

Open and shut,
This case: the Lord
Jumped overboard,
Fell while rock climbing,
Or died two-timing
His better half;
His rod and staff
Won't come for me.

Of course, to be
Fair, sitting here
Partly sincere
And partly pissed,
I might have missed
A whispered word.

I'd have preferred
The whirlwind, Lord.

THE CLOUD OF WITNESSES THROUGH WINTER AIR:

I wage the combat with two mighty foes,
Which are more strong than I ten thousand fold;
The one is when thy pleasure I do lose,
The other, when thy person I behold.

With how sad steps, Oh Moon, thou climbst the skies,
How silently, and with how wan a face!
Your pulse is failing, Passion speechless lies;
I read it in thy looks, thy languished grace,

Feeling forthwith the other burning power.
Do not, O do not, from poor me remove
This close-companioned inarticulate hour
When twofold silence is the song of love!

Fresh shalt thou see in me the wounds thou madest,
Though spent thy flame, in me the heat remaining,
I that have loved thee thus before thou fadest;
My faith shall wax, when thou art in thy waning.

AN OLD MAN ROCKING IN A ROCKING CHAIR:

The world is too much with us, late and soon.
We are as clouds that veil the midnight moon.
Out, out, brief candle. Brightly as you may,
You cannot burn much longer anyway.

*

I cherish this old cut
Of "Just a Closer Walk with Thee"

Done à la Dixieland . . . A one, two, three
   And the whole band has caught

   The spirit, sweet and swinging;
  They skip the bebop razzmatazz
And riff on earlier, earthier types of jazz.
   Although there's no one singing,

   The clarinetist plays
  The melody, or something close
Enough (plus grace notes, bends, arpeggios,
   And trills) that he implies

   The words. The trumpet wawls,
  The tuba farts, the trombone slides
Through long, chromatic, comical asides,
   The grainy fiddle drawls

   A few droll, down-home phrases—
  The fruit of all the improv skills
I lack in spite of practicing my scales—
   And it's one huge ekphrasis,

   An audible mosaic
  Insisting that without a text
Or any certainty of what comes next,
   I finally face the music.

       *

A boy beneath a blue and cloudless sky
   Stands barefoot in a field
And tips his head back, giddy with the scents
   Of grass and dark rich earth

Beneath his heels. He doesn't wonder why
The goodness of the world has been revealed
     In all its imminence,
Nor does he question its intrinsic worth.

His eyes are closed. He spins in circles, feels
     The breeze across his cheek,
And breathes in deep, rejoicing in his lungs;
     Then, head aswim, he sinks
Down to the grass and listens to the peals
Of birdsong as the wrens and redwings speak
     In charismatic tongues:
O taste and see! Plus hear, smell, touch! he thinks.

Eyes still closed, he slowly turns his head,
     Scanning the unseen sky,
And senses the direction of the sun
     By how it warms his face
And floods his field of vision with bright red—
His eyelids' blood. He dreams he'll never die
     And feels himself at one
With earth, birds, grass, and sky. I call that grace.

Whatever part of me that might believe
     This sensate scene too gaudy
For real belief, that never would intuit
     A god I couldn't find
In cloisters of the mind—grant a reprieve
To that blessed child, that he might trust his body
     While trying to see through it,
As opening his eyes would leave him blind.

*

Through all the endless baiting and debating,
Backbiting, betting, biding, and upbraiding,
Forbidding, aiding and abetting, fretting,
Confiding, fighting, thwarting fate, and fading,
I wonder which of us is truly waiting.

*

Follow that couple home. The sirens fade,
But other sounds surround them: techno music,
Beer bottle clinks, drunk laughter. Someone sobs
And blows her nose. They wander past a blazing
Convenience store; the clerk there brought his laptop
To work and downloads porn until the door
Swings open and a customer comes in
To buy another bottle of cheap red wine;
The clerk pretends he's playing online games.

The downtown noise grows faint as they near home.
The air is brisk. They hear the aimless rustling
Of fallen leaves and empty paper bags
Blowing across the streets, and when they sigh,
Their separate breaths emerge as thin, white clouds
That mingle, dissipate, and drift away.
The jazz quartet they caught tonight was hot
And even played "Someday My Prince Will Come,"
Her favorite. *But I'm here!* he always jokes.

The porch steps creak. Once they're inside, she sees
The huge bouquet of roses on the table;
It is their anniversary. Eight years.
One of these days they really will get married;
For now, they live together. As he checks

The answering machine, she reads his card,
Twirling the ringlets that tickle down her neck.
His college roommate called, inviting him
To watch a church-league softball game tomorrow.

They head upstairs, undress for bed, and lie
Next to each other, reading magazines.
His has an article about Hipparchus,
The ancient astronomer who catalogued
Over eight hundred objects in the sky;
Who could perhaps predict solar eclipses;
And most importantly, who first described
Precession, earth's slow wobble on its axis,
Which makes our polestar change as time goes by.

The man is restless. Next he tries to read
A work of popular theology
But finds himself rereading one quotation:
Spiritus Sanctus non est scepticus.
"You mind if I turn on the television?"
He asks the woman. "Go ahead," she murmurs.
He starts with news, but all of it is bad:
A local sex offender tried and sentenced,
A drug-related murder, more statistics.

He flips the channel to a talk show rerun;
A spirited stand-up comic is explaining,
"My best impressions end up being myself,
Or versions of myself, except they sound
Like other people and are hilarious!"
He flips the channel. Now a pudgy man
Sporting a pompadour and perfect teeth

Leans back behind a table piled with money.
Text scrolls across the bottom of the screen:

To make a covenant with God call now.
It brings to mind a Tallahassee preacher
He heard once on the radio: "God wants
A people who are desperate. Are you *desperate*?
Tell him you want the *Word*!" The man remembers
His last Palm Sunday in his Baptist church:
The children's pastor made the preschool kids
Spread their palm branches on the floor midaisle
And yell, "Hosanna!" Jesus didn't enter,

Of course, and afterward he'd helped to vacuum
The sanctuary floor, but the image stuck;
Whenever he's grown sick of seeking God,
He's thought of all those kids lined up. He says,
"Tell me you love me."
                              "If you make me tell you,
Nothing I say will make you think it's true,"
She answers, and she pauses. "But I love you."
She takes his hand in hers and turns it over
To kiss him on the wrist. His stomach flutters.

One time he asked his father how he knew
His mother was the one. His father said,
"We spent an evening sitting on the porch swing
In complete silence. Never spoke a word.
It struck me as the deepest conversation
I'd ever had. At last, your mother said,
You hear that? 'What?' I asked. I knew we'd settled

Into a rhythm, breathing side by side.
Now that's the sound of trust, she said. I knew."

Picture our man roll over. Hear him mumble
"Good night" and wait for her to dim the lamp.
Good night, sweet prince, good night, she doesn't say.
She reads. He hears the pages crackle, breathe,
Then thwap against the floor. The lights go out.
You cannot see this, but beneath the covers
She rubs his shoulder, then glides down his arm.
She doesn't take his hand; she waits for him.
He braids their fingers, and they kiss in silence.

Notes

Upon First Viewing Ball of Fire

At the end of the scene alluded to here, Gene Krupa lights the matchsticks he has been percussing with, holds them up, and he and Barbara Stanwyck blow them out.

Elegy for Paul deLay

Paul deLay was a Portland-based blues musician and one of the most innovative harmonica players of the past forty years. The anecdote in the second section of this poem is true: although this shouldn't matter to the success of the poem, I hope it helps confirm that Paul deLay was a kind and gracious man. His last album is indeed a live album, and the penultimate track features words from him much like the ones used here.

Dracula *in Spanish: Imitations of Immortality*

As befits a poem about vampirism, I have cannibalized several other poems. Sources are as follows:

> line 20: Tennyson, "Tithonus"
> lines 35–36: John 15:13
> line 61: Larkin, "An Arundel Tomb"
> line 70: Milton, *Paradise Lost*
> line 77: Shakespeare, Sonnet 29
> line 81: Elizabeth Barrett Browning, Sonnet 43
> line 90: Elizabeth Barrett Browning, Sonnet 1
> lines 95–96: Keats, "When I Have Fears"

The actress who played Eva was Lupita Tovar.